Kim and the Kid

By Sally Cowan

Kim got up
and ran to Gab's pen.

The kids ran to Gab.

She fed her kids.

But a kid did not get up.

It had a bad leg.

"We can go to Quin
the vet!" said Dad.

Kim got in Dad's big van.

The kid sat in a rug
on Kim's lap.

At the vet,
the kid got a jab.

The kid's leg has a cut.

The kid sat on Quin's lap.

It got fed.

It had lots of sips.

Sip, sip, sip!

"Look!" said Kim.

"The kid can get up!"

CHECKING FOR MEANING

1. What is the mother goat's name? *(Literal)*

2. Why did Kim and her dad take one of the kids to the vet? *(Literal)*

3. What might have happened if they didn't take the kid to the vet? *(Inferential)*

EXTENDING VOCABULARY

Gab's	Look at the word *Gab's*. What are the apostrophe and *s* on the end of the word showing? Find other words in the text that end in *s*.
kids	The word *kids* means baby goats. What other meaning does the word *kids* have?
lap	Look at the word *lap*. How many sounds are in it?

MOVING BEYOND THE TEXT

1. What other animals might Kim and her dad keep on the farm?

2. A kid is a baby goat. What other words for baby animals do you know?

3. What do you think happened when the baby goat got back to the farm?

4. What are some other places where animals are kept and cared for by people?

SPEED SOUNDS

Kk   Ll   Vv   Qq   Ww

Dd   Jj   Oo   Gg   Uu

Cc   Bb   Rr   Ee   Ff   Hh   Nn

Mm   Ss   Aa   Pp   Ii   Tt

PRACTICE WORDS

kid

Quin

leg

van

vet

lap

lots

Kim

kids